In the Garden of Old Age

Poetry by Nina Freedlander Gibans

Photography by Abby Star

In the Garden of Old Age

Poetry by Nina Freedlander Gibans

Photography by Abby Star

Copyright © 2019

3rd Printing

ISBN — 9781626131071

Published by ATBOSH Media ltd.

Cleveland, Ohio, USA

http://www.atbosh.com

Dedicated to

Lois Freedlander

at 103 years

Lois Freedlander

103 years young

Leans into her 103rd

Still plays bridge, does daily crossword puzzles

And watches baseball. Lifetime sport

Banks on math skills

Keeps roots alive on a tree starting to lean.

Keeps them vibrant and green

In their spring and her winter.

The four corners of the table
Wheelchairs on the angle
stories new to new friends
Dried as raisins to the old friend
Half remembered by an acquaintance
They dribble like basketballs ready for the dunk
Glyphics for interpretation, with forks and spoons
They are the world this moment
Tales of vintage clothes, connections
Of former neighbors 60 years ago,
Unknown then, but how...
A musician, airline stewardess, educator in one small frail
Frame, two art historians whose meeting is the jelly on the bread
A former nurse "hold your arms up if you are choking."
The wisdom of teabags to heat sore skin, salves for the soul,
Ice cream made for aging nerves - moose tracks with chocolate sauce
Consignments, fertile ground for digging into the past.
The women's wear vintage outfit
Specializing in one piece garments took my two piece clothes without a whimper.
Every day takes a turn with the past, people from a yesterday or years past.
Vintage meant 90s – is that really "over the hill" or yesterday?

Kaddish

These poems were written and published by Tupelo Press during August and September 2018 as part of their 30/30 Project. The rest were written this winter and many winters ago.

For every voice there is a silence. For every person there are voices and silences. For every voice and every silence there are memories. The Kaddish is the prayer traditionally recited in memory of the dead although it makes no mention of death. It's found in daily prayer services. Unknowingly we remember daily mostly in silence.

Then memory spills into conversations

Yesterday-At tables questions circulate with many and no answers

Hearing portions of sentences, parts of words, eyeball translating

Today--Voices towards thin air and expressions--Twisted eyebrows, cupped ears, pensive eyes behind big rims, battered minds, they knew but do not know now, they laughed but now smile crookedly, they eat small bites and ice cream, baffled by knives and forks or spoons which is which and for what foods? Folding napkins is a full occupation. Mismatched socks, shirts for summer worn in winter, Where am I?

Yesterday--On the edge years away? Is my color grey or brown or pink following the stripe on life's highway. Am I going West with Keroac to Africa or Nebraska with Kingsolver, Chicago with Bellows, New York with Roth, countryside with Lyndon and Babette? Up from the South with Wilkerson? I am lucky I can travel in my mind. Where am I?

Today--The receptionist sings information calmly interpreting inquiries with more than two hands and three phones.

Tonight the New Year brought 15 assorted grandchildren home on vacation assorted ages some facing the blank expressions of who they were.

Blue eyes meet brown eyes; green eyes meet on a fitness trail prepared for canes, wheelchairs, slow walkers, wanderers as they pass windows with news of weather, branches bending with the wind slightly or energetically. Natives of Asia or So. Africa; India and Brooklyn, Wooster, San Francisco, Iowa meet historians, scientists, doctors, artists, teachers, librarians meld with years together researching new lives together. Card players win daily bond lose or win over Uno, Rummy, Bridge. Masters of past minds in math, chemistry, and arts.

Flutes, pianos, voices mix in melody in the hallways. Corridors of the mind remember husbands, wives and troubles. Everyone's troubles are in the attic of their lives.

Yesterday--Displacements and placements. Was it by the cherry tree? The blue flowers by the gate? I remember dahlias –the suns of days that grew them. Displacements and new spring smells, mixed with remembered purple shrubs at the old house. Time evaporated into light and dark –shadows motion us gliding through patches of grey and distinct color.

Today--The dining table is a tiny community. One likes the comics, sports and bridge sections of the newspaper, another likes Science Tuesday, another likes politics and commentary and the fourth likes the Arts and Entertainment. Delivery systems haven't worked; sharing what we do receive among us does.

Yesterday one did yoga, the next went to movies, the next paid bills and the fourth went to a gallery. They walked, traveled by wheelchair, and car. We shared notes. The gallery won. The paintings were meditative and processed beautifully.

Today walking a fine line to keep balance; don't we all?

Yesterday we were upright.

Tomorrow ….we are all still here

Yesterday we were with artists—many artists with different abstractions of themselves. We think we do not understand abstraction – we stand far away against the shadows of the room and see outlines and hear sounds and voices…

Today we talked though our teeth about what's going on around us.

Yesterday satisfaction begot calm; there are ripples in our lives everywhere.

Our memories are our salvation; whatever and wherever they break through the day.

They are like our museum of experience; if we don't care for one, moving on is best

This is Kaddish.

Life

I missed the opera, the baseball game, lunch

A movie, yes, Forrest Gump stayed by a broken machine

Waiting for anyone anyone ANYONE smarter than I am about

INTERNET down up collusion connection turn off turn on three times

The magic number today is not even the 13th.

I will have a glass of wine to the future.

Going to a concert after 70 years

I counted the heads of grey

All natural --- celebrating habits of music

This was Shostakovich their contemporary

Writing in joy of life, fear of death, speaking

To toe tappers, former dancers. active thinkers

 Friends for all 70 years --- music scores

A real audience listening through hearing aids,

Penetrating deaf ears with new vigor –beat and vigor

Pulsing –musicians joyful at their work, smiling.

Life

Raking through our pile of Fall leaves
burying joys that once were
Puppies nibble at our heels and buoy us
Digging into our own success
(and everyone has a secret one)
My color may be maple red or sun yellow
Or flat tan. What is yours?

For Richard

Cranial creases

Beautiful lines

    Shape

    Creative thinking

        In oranges, yellows, reds

        A little purple.

            New forms like old friends

          we see and we remember.

              grey stone

              softened

                  by years of kindness.

Richard was a major ceramic artist.

For Jim

Pearl grey music now

Solemn low sterno

Bach's ostinato too drilling

Mahler too expansive

Gillespie perfect

I've lived with every one of their works

Heard them daily

Mooring my thoughts, anchoring the hours.

Jim was a respected architect.

For Marge

Folding my napkin simplifies my life

I have almost finished

My meal is too much

It wraps my life neatly

Into the squares

eight children unwrapped my days

Stirring the soups.

Marge was a stewardess, singer, educator and had nine children.

For Helen

Gently forcefully

softly, deftly she walks her days

mindfully.

The roses get water, the birds are fed

the readings in the papers; we throw up our hands.

She is capable of handling almost anything

But...

Helen headed the Art History department of a college.

For Eugenia

I am Russian

Packaged with stories

About my past and holocaust heritage

Like my missing bags relatives memories

Deleted from my lifetext.

I have been here nearly 40 years

And learn new things every one of my days

Lectures, music, especially Boris Godunov

Eugenia came from Russia years ago and does needlework

For Jane

Shares stories graciously
Introduces friends to be sure we know
Each other each day every day
Red lipstick and rims for glasses
Brightening her day and ours.

Jane lived across the street.

For Dorothy

Since the "elementary school" of my life,

Her performances have made my day, my year,

When she performs, she brings life to this day

Fresh with the vigor of 90 year-old youth

Pathos and feisty energy catching the stars of the years

For all of us.

Dorothy is a major actress.

For Blanche

Creator of lines

Shaped

Small sculptures

Pendants for women

Fractured by age

Gloried by color for the queens in all of us.

Blanche was an artist specializing in jewelry design.

For Beth

the sound of words
against the found idea
matted against surrounding
music, maybe?

Beth was an English teacher.

For Jim

Lying under the skin of night light

I listen to the music we both hear even now

It keeps you here with me

The shadows of light and night

Defined our future and leave me to define mine.

For Irene

Sitting at lunch
With the discussants of today
daily glee club practices in a living room
sang again;
ice cream melting from Ben and Jerry, Mitchells, Honey Hut
dripping over the years
chocolate drizzle, coffee mocha, mint-laced
tongues licking our words.

Irene knows the words to all old songs.

For Mary

Hand in the cookie jar

Now it's her turn to snitch

With the whole room watching.

Leftovers from childhood

"smarts" and innocence

How many times has the hand

Been in the jar?

Now no one would mind

Since she does it with practice and grace.

Mary always knew better.

For those who can see

The hallways are trails

like former forest paths

Bird feeders for the clan of sparrows

who can smell the roses too.

Friends reading, helping each other see or hear

The chatter.

Everyone goes to their rooms or trees until tomorrow.

For Nancy

Heart in music
Heart in painting
Heart In storytelling
Hearts anyone?

Nancy was a nurse.

For the dogs that visit

Molly slow and sleek

Oscar just plain comfortable

Lucy a true lap dog

Fur soft as new fuzz on an old dog

All like the treat I have

The secret of my success

And I get to pet them.

A place for everyone

Sunday is "Times" day

for those who still read;

Big screen day

for those who can still hear

memory café day to help us remember

the stories we may have laid aside for awhile

waiting for a new audience.

Can you hear them?

A place for mastering one's soul

Mastering one's soul is easiest when

Memories return non sequitur and we spend time—

all the time—sorting them for self summaries

that hold us steady moving us onward

peacefully.

Fretful confrontation easiest in dreams

that disappear with daylight

Disagree with daylight

Sometimes reappearing the next night.

A place for pleasantries and honest talk

My corner room is a forest, a meadow, the lake

If I look far enough

a "Central Park" in Ohio,

my neighborhood when a car passes

on the city street below.

A place for resting

The bid for seeds

Send restive sparrows to the ground

For the spill from the foraging squirrel

The governing cardinal, the gossiping jay.

This is a busy place,

Fawns and Moms come to see

Then saunter elsewhere

Of greater interest.

A place for seeing color

That same patio

is best for looking at color

picked for a piece of memory

or to renew spirit

bright red flowers in large planters

roses good enough to drive away doldrums

dark green trees home to nests,

light green planted leaves primed by sun and rain,

mid green ground cloth on a slope

reflecting this year's moisture

perfect vision for imperfect eyes

more than a quick glance

only gained by sitting quietly daily.

A place for peace

Turning the leaves of books

Turning the corners of the years

Turning time with times

Turning from sun to shade

Turning in tune with the wind

Turning a mind full of gains and losses

Turning the pages again and again.

A place for peace

A straggling piece of life's cloth

    Just a bit left to sew the hem

        You fill the patchwork

            Of colors and cottons

                (or velvets for life's best moments.)

            Soft and lush

            A few course strands

        For the raw textures that are interspersed.

        I can feel moments through these threads

And move to smooth them now.

For Margaret

At 105 she can pick my flowers anytime.

She knows how to do it right

As the gardener she was. Her eyes

See anything brown

She and the colors melt into the sun.

They are her private treasure.

Margaret was a masterful gardener

A place for mournings

Is there such a thing as grace with pain?

edges unraveling

knotting speech

Blunting senses,

Cutting vision

And hunger.

Inside there are always tears.

A place for the best we are

On the other hand (as Jewish people say)

We've been fed the best for many years

Had yogurt and prime rib

Looked at health and squared with it

Ice cream and roses ... all I ever wanted

It was a good life-choice

What's your fancy?

For Marilyn B.

In August the most orange month

With sun rays hot and heavy in our summer of demise

Beautiful plants stand tall and steady

facing certain Fall. They have faced the storms

survived wet and cold.

They have danced with the wind, floated petals

of love like Venetian glass angled in the sun.

Everyone has a choice of being a purple lilac of Spring

or dahlias of August

You are an August dahlia!

Marilyn has been a dancer and introduced
                              this community to the beauty of craft.

A place for peace

Different from sudden attacks forcing
us into a new way of breathing,
we mourn even before it is officially mourning time
when people are not who they were
and don't know who they are.
We climb the mountain of years between us
gasping for air, struggling for words, and hope.
We are autonomous robots of our own making
our thinking crowds between memory and action
narrow passageways small turns big breaths
Simmering against life itself.

A place for peace

Each garden is perennial

Striking a compromise between the lilies and groundcover

Perfect portraits of flowerhood or earth-bound green.

Each one of us has a chosen place, a duration, a compromise

A life prepared and unprepared for taking chances,

This garden is special

Are you a rose today, azalea tomorrow?

I can smell dianthus to begin my day

Bougainvilleas from a trip to Spain

Imagine lilacs all year round

Bring sunflowers to the conversation

My family gardeners have saved my soul.

A place for peace

From an old Irish hymn

      Wake, now, my senses, on this thirtieth day

      Senses surrounding silvery grief

      Frame my tomorrow in a new way

      Wake, now my reason, as I head to September

      With Fall's palette of colorful leaf

      Wake, now, compassion, and then remember

      To honor August's garden at this fragile time

      Buttressed by friendships, and feelings aligned.

150 Years of Faces

150 years of faces, a quilt of photos
laid out upon my bed
I have met some of them
on shelves, sleeves in the wedding albums
in the back of the old scrapbook
marking a part in the Hagaddah.

They are on the piano, on the bookcase
on the cart, on the table in front of the window.
My grandfather sits in a grand frame on the floor;
my grandmother is on the wall
hair swept up regal and blond
above her high collar
just like a famous portrait
by a famous artist.

Now I need more; What was she like

holding that baby, my grandmother?

I do not know them; I did not hug them.

My father tried to tell me

how they lived when they came

to settle here from Poland;

stories stumble from the pictures

relatives and friends tell theirs.

Sentences end in old lilac bushes, in the deep antique rose,

in the trail of wisteria perfume,

mulled cinnamon, clove and winter spices

old recipes in my grandmother's handwriting.

I cannot know unless I am told;

I cannot believe unless I know;

I cannot hug them unless they are in my dreams

And I am in the pictures with them.

At the Museum

Yesterday

I got lost, on a two-lane road

when I was supposed to turn.

For 11 miles, I shared space with one biker

until he disappeared in the seat of the valley,

body hunched to the road. I passed him. No cars,

tree-forms in the yellow harvest

brown guideposts; wheat waiting to be cut.

Today at the museum

minefield of labels, images stalking the words

I want to talk back to the painting,

It was a purple road, and the biker's cap was yellow.

meadow sprinkle of nasturtium on salad greens;

wheat bending like a paintbrush; I was a painter

it was our space.

Yesterday

real perspective, orange sun on the window

through side streets, and decay

Today

I look at paintings, and remember

to celebrate survival.

Withering

Three weeks six deaths

Friends alive when seen a month ago or in memory

Hunched over life laughing at themselves

Unknowing -- they had no way of knowing truth

Waiting for the other sock out of the wash

Waiting for rubber bands to hold their sides together

Waiting to argue

Waiting to tell time

Waiting to know night from day

Waiting in line.

About the Poet

Nina Freedlander Gibans has never allowed the challenges of cerebral palsy to stand in the way of anything she wished to achieve. Called an "arts visionary and assiduous arts advocate" by the Cleveland Arts Prize, which awarded her their 2009 Martha Joseph Prize, Gibans has been widely celebrated for her work as a community arts leader and educator. She has been a board member of the Cleveland Artists Foundation (now ARTneo), the Cleveland Chamber Music Society, Cleveland City Club, and The Shaker Heights Public Library and developed many collaborative city-wide community projects. Gibans has launched numerous projects and organizations, collaborating to establish strong foundations for their sustainability and longevity. She has documented her initiatives in multiple films, books, and educational websites as a way of spreading knowledge widely. Having published books of her own poetry, Gibans also worked to have a street named for her region's poet laureate. In June of 2018, she published her eighth book, *Celebrating the Soul of Cleveland*.

Some Context...

Poetry has been a life venture for Nina.

• At Laurel School. Her translations from Latin and in English class went mostly unappreciated.

• In the presence of poets her entire life. Including studies with Horace Gregory (Sarah Lawrence College), Louis Zukofsky (San Francisco Poetry Center), Vincent McHugh (San Francisco — Retired chair of Federal Writing Project, NYC), a workshop with Alicia Ostriker, and communication with Naomi Shihab Nye, Robert Pinsky, Alberta Turner. Friend of Richard

Howard, Cleveland native Pulitzer Prize MacArthur Award winner.— encouraging encounters.

• Read in San Francisco as part of the group working with Vincent McHugh in bars and on the stage as a fore-act to Allen Ginsberg's performance.

• Active with Poet's League of Cleveland.

• Publications: *And So I Must Imagine* (XLibris 2009). Co-editor with Mary Weems and Larry Smith of Cleveland Poetry Scenes: *A Panorama and Anthology* (Bottom Dog Press 2008) Piloted at John Hay High School and Shaker Heights Middle School and Cleveland Public Libraries. *18 Gardens and their Gardeners* with Michael Loderstedt, photographer, 1999 an Ohio Arts Council Art Project Grant. *Rosepetals...towards memory* (ATBOSH Media Ltd.)

• Taught creative writing at The Cleveland Museum of Art in East Cleveland arts project.

• Co-Director, *Silver Apples of the Moon* project asking for community response to poetry and art — with Shaker Heights Public Library, Cleveland Public Library, & The Cleveland Museum of Art, & the. Book edited by Neal Chandler, Cleveland State University.

• Read in museums, bookstores, and libraries in Cleveland.

> "we are connected underneath the seafloor of our psyches" from *Poetry and Healing: Some Moments of Wholeness* by Alicia Ostriker in the *American Poetry Review*, March/April 2018.

About the Photographer

Abby Star is a native of Cleveland, Ohio. She received her BA in Studio Art from Carleton College in Minnesota. During her time at Carleton, Abby worked as a Teaching Assistant for various photography classes, in both digital and film photography. Following graduation, she returned to Carleton for an extra year to work as an Educational Associate in the Studio Art Department as well as to photograph Carleton's permanent art collection. Abby has had work featured in shows in both Cleveland and Minnesota.

Abby's photography journey began in high school with her first black and white film photography class. While she still loves film photography, she currently primarily works with digital photography these days. Historically, her work has focused on nature- specifically trees and flowers. More recently, experimentation and manipulation have become central components of her work. She also enjoys photographing at night and using lights to manipulate the subject of the photograph. It is the ability to control the lighting and to use the lighting to manipulate an image that have, in part, drawn her to increasingly shoot at night.

In her free time, Abby likes to spend time with her dog, Bailey, a Chihuahua-beagle mix, as well as dance, read and play board games.